NOAA: Initial Response to Post-Storm Assessment Requirements

July 11, 2013

Congressional Committees

NOAA: Initial Response to Post-Storm Assessment Requirements

After a hurricane, assessing damage caused by different perils, such as high winds or flooding, is especially challenging when all that is left after the storm is a structure's foundation. For these properties, there may not be enough physical evidence to determine the extent to which damage was caused by wind versus flooding. Private property-casualty insurers typically cover wind damage but exclude coverage for flood damage. The National Flood Insurance Program, administered by the Department of Homeland Security's Federal Emergency Management Agency (FEMA), provides federally backed coverage for flood damage. After the hurricane season in 2005, legal disputes arose between private property-casualty insurers and policyholders over interpretation of policy language that excluded coverage of damage caused concurrently or sequentially by a covered peril—wind—and an excluded peril—flooding.

The Consumer Option for an Alternative System to Allocate Losses Act of 2012 (COASTAL Act)[1] addresses the compilation and use of scientific data to help FEMA allocate losses related to wind and flooding after major storms for certain properties. The act requires the Department of Commerce's National Oceanic and Atmospheric Administration (NOAA) to generate post-storm assessments within 90 days of certain tropical storms or hurricanes for FEMA's use in a standard formula for allocating such losses.[2] To generate the post-storm assessments, NOAA is required by the COASTAL Act to develop a post-storm model by regulation by December 28, 2013, that replicates wind speeds, storm surge heights, and other measurements for these storms. The act requires a certain degree of accuracy for both the post-storm assessment and post-storm model. For example, the post-storm model must be designed to generate post-storm assessments that have a degree of accuracy of not less than 90 percent for every specific property loss for which it is utilized. The act does not define 90 percent accuracy and does not specify how to measure it.

---

[1]Pub. L. No. 112-141, Div. F, Tit. II, Subtit. B, 126 Stat. 405, 969 (2012).

[2]Specifically, the act requires NOAA to generate these assessments for "named" storms that the NOAA Administrator, in consultation with the Secretary of Homeland Security, determines may reasonably constitute a threat to any portion of a coastal state. The act defines a named storm as any organized weather system with a defined surface circulation and maximum winds of at least 39 miles per hour that NOAA's National Weather Service names a tropical storm or hurricane. According to NOAA officials, the act did not fully capture the official NOAA criteria used when categorizing and naming tropical storms and hurricanes (i.e., tropical cyclones), which requires maximum sustained winds of 39 miles per hour or greater. NOAA officials told us that the agency will continue to follow its criteria in naming these types of storms. A coastal state is defined as a U.S. state in, or bordering on, the Atlantic, Pacific, or Arctic Ocean, the Gulf of Mexico, Long Island Sound, or one or more of the Great Lakes and includes the U.S. territories.

NOAA, in consultation with the Office of the Federal Coordinator for Meteorology (OFCM),[3] also is to identify federal and state efforts, as well as domestic private and academic efforts, that are capable of collecting the weather data (i.e., covered data) necessary to develop the post-storm model and assessment, evaluate their coverage gaps, and report to Congress a plan for collecting the covered data.[4]

The act mandates GAO to audit federal efforts to collect covered data.[5] During our review, NOAA was in the process of developing the post-storm model and determining which data collection efforts would be required. Based on discussions with the relevant committees, we determined our objectives were to examine (1) storm data collection efforts that NOAA has identified that may provide the covered data for the COASTAL Act storm model and (2) the extent to which selected federal agencies collect cost information on their storm data collection efforts. On May 29, 2013, we briefed you (see encl. I) on our overall findings, which are also reflected in this report, concerning federal efforts to collect covered data to address the mandate.

To examine storm data collection efforts that NOAA has identified, we reviewed COASTAL Act planning documents from an interagency work group that included NOAA and other agencies—the Department of the Interior's U.S. Geological Survey (USGS), the U.S. Army Corps of Engineers (the Corps), the National Aeronautics and Space Administration (NASA), and FEMA. We interviewed officials from NOAA and these other agencies, as well as the Department of Homeland Security's U.S. Coast Guard and OFCM. We also interviewed representatives from a university, a nonprofit organization, and a private company about their storm data collection efforts because they were identified in the COASTAL Act planning documents and during interviews with the federal agencies.

To examine the extent to which selected agencies collect cost information on their storm data collection efforts, we selected NOAA and USGS to focus on because these agencies had certain data collection efforts that agency officials told us would likely be an important source of covered data. We reviewed budget and financial documentation for fiscal years 2012 and 2013 provided by NOAA and USGS for their storm data collection efforts. We also interviewed agency officials from these two agencies to identify the type of cost information available for these agencies' storm data collection efforts.

We conducted this performance audit from September 2012 to July 2013 in accordance with generally accepted government auditing standards. Those standards require that we plan and perform the audit to obtain sufficient, appropriate evidence to provide a reasonable basis for our findings and conclusions based on our audit objectives. We believe that the evidence obtained provides a reasonable basis for our findings and conclusions based on our audit objectives.

---

[3]OFCM is an interdepartmental office, within the Department of Commerce, established in 1964 to coordinate federal meteorological activities among various agencies.

[4]Covered data are defined by the act as data collected before, during, or after named storms and necessary to determine magnitude and timing of wind speeds, rainfall, barometric pressure, and river flows; the extent, height, and timing of storm surge; topographic (land shape) and bathymetric (ocean depth) data; and other measures.

[5]Pub. L. No. 112-141, Div. F, Tit. II, Subtit. B, § 100252, 126 Stat. 405, 974 (2012). The act requires GAO to submit a report on its audit findings by July 6, 2013 (1 year after enactment of the act).

In summary, NOAA, in consultation with OFCM and other agencies, has identified federal and nonfederal storm data collection efforts that may provide the covered data for the COASTAL Act storm model. However, NOAA officials told us they will not know which specific efforts will be used until they develop the post-storm model. According to agency officials and representatives from nonfederal entities, efforts that can collect surface level water, wave, and wind measurements over land will likely provide important sources of data for the model. NOAA and USGS, as well as some nonfederal entities such as universities and private companies, currently collect some surface level data on wind and water. However, these officials and representatives said current efforts may not be sufficient for the model to achieve the highly accurate estimates needed for individual structures in all locations. For example, USGS officials said they may not have enough mobile, temporary water level sensors to deploy in locations along the Atlantic Coast for measuring storm tide.[6] Moreover, officials from NOAA, USGS, and the Corps told us that current efforts do not measure certain types of data that likely will be needed to model wind and water impacts on individual structures. These officials said that, in particular, data on waves that occur over land on top of the storm surge are critical for assessing water damage to structures from tropical storms and hurricanes but are not currently collected. NOAA officials told us that, among their next steps in planning for meeting the requirements of the COASTAL Act, the agency will be examining how to fill the gaps they identified in current storm data collection efforts.

The selected agencies we reviewed—NOAA and USGS—do not typically collect cost information on specific types of storm or weather data, such as wind speed, that reflects the expense for all activities involved in collecting and using the data. Officials from NOAA and USGS told us that their storm data collection efforts typically collect multiple types of storm or weather data and that the costs for processing, analyzing, and storing the data are calculated for all data types rather than a single one. Agencies then incorporate the cost information they do collect on their storm data collection efforts into the costs of major programs and projects, such as responding to a major hurricane. For example, one NOAA official said cost information is collected under the agency's Tides and Currents program for all data collected by the National Water Level Observation Network (NWLON) and another effort called the Physical Oceanographic Real-Time System (PORTS). NWLON collects water level data at the U.S. coastline and PORTS collects water and weather data in some U.S. ports and harbors. In addition, USGS officials told us they collected detailed cost information on activities related to collecting data on storm tide, barometric pressure, and high water mark levels during Hurricane Sandy. NOAA officials said that, as a next step in its COASTAL Act planning, the agency plans to prepare a resource analysis that is to, in part, identify some of the additional resources needed to fill gaps in storm data collection efforts. At the time of our review, a NOAA official told us that the agency did not know when the resource analysis would be completed because the agency officials involved in COASTAL Act planning were still deliberating on the post-storm model and the data collection efforts that will be required for this model.

We are not making any recommendations in this report.

---

[6]USGS installs these sensors along the shoreline and a short distance inland to supplement permanent water level sensors. According to USGS officials, there are 300 sensors distributed among USGS offices in most of the coastal states to facilitate rapid deployment 48 to 24 hours prior to a major storm's landfall. Storm tide is water level rise due to the combination of storm surge and the normal high tide.

Agency Comments

We provided a draft of this report to officials from the Departments of Commerce, Defense, Homeland Security, and the Interior; NASA; and OFCM for their review and comment. Commerce and the Interior provided technical comments, which we incorporated as appropriate. The other agencies we reviewed had no comments.

--- --- --- --- ---

We are sending copies of this report to the Secretaries of Commerce, Defense, Homeland Security, and the Interior; the Administrator of NASA; the Federal Coordinator for Meteorology; the appropriate congressional committees; and other interested parties. In addition, the report is available at no charge on the GAO website at http://www.gao.gov.

If you or your staff members have any questions concerning this report, please contact me at (202) 512-3841 or fennella@gao.gov. Contact points for our Offices of Congressional Relations and Public Affairs may be found on the last page of this report. GAO staff who made key contributions to this report are listed in enclosure II.

Anne-Marie Fennell
Director, Natural Resources and Environment

Enclosures—II

List of Committees

The Honorable Tim Johnson
Chairman
The Honorable Mike Crapo
Ranking Member
Committee on Banking, Housing, and Urban Affairs
United States Senate

The Honorable Jay Rockefeller
Chairman
The Honorable John Thune
Ranking Member
Committee on Commerce, Science, and Transportation
United States Senate

The Honorable Jeb Hensarling
Chairman
The Honorable Maxine Waters
Ranking Member
Committee on Financial Services
House of Representatives

The Honorable Lamar Smith
Chairman
The Honorable Eddie Bernice Johnson
Ranking Member
Committee on Science, Space, and Technology
House of Representatives

GAO

NOAA: Initial Response to Post-Storm Assessment Requirements

Briefing for Congressional Committees

May 29, 2013, revised June 28, 2013

Page 1

 **GAO**

Introduction

- Hurricanes pose challenges for insurers and property owners because they cause damage from multiple perils, such as high winds and flooding. Assessing such damage is especially challenging when all that is left after the storm is a structure's foundation. For these properties, there may not be enough physical evidence to determine the extent to which damage was caused by wind versus flooding.

- Private property-casualty insurers typically cover wind damage but exclude coverage for flood damage. The National Flood Insurance Program (NFIP), administered by the Federal Emergency Management Agency (FEMA), provides federally backed coverage for flood damage.

- After the hurricane season in 2005, legal disputes arose between private property-casualty insurers and policyholders over interpretation of policy language that excluded coverage of damage caused concurrently or sequentially by a covered peril—wind—and an excluded peril—flooding.

Page 2

Introduction
(Continued)

- The Consumer Option for an Alternative System to Allocate Losses Act of 2012 (COASTAL Act)[1] addresses the compilation and use of scientific data to help FEMA allocate losses related to wind and flooding after major storms for certain properties (i.e., indeterminate losses).

- Under the act, indeterminate losses are those arising from flooding and wind associated with a named storm where an adjuster certified under the NFIP,[2] in consultation with an engineer, as appropriate, determines for that specific property there (1) are no material remnants except the building foundation and (2) is insufficient or no tangible evidence as a result of the named storm.

[1]The act was enacted along with other provisions reauthorizing and reforming the NFIP within the Moving Ahead for Progress in the 21st Century Act. Pub. L. No. 112-141, Div. F, Tit. II, Subtit. B, 126 Stat. 405, 969 (2012).

[2]Specifically, the act defines a "named storm" as any organized weather system with a defined surface circulation and maximum winds of at least 39 miles per hour that the National Weather Service of the National Oceanic and Atmospheric Administration (NOAA) names a tropical storm or hurricane. According to NOAA officials, the act did not fully capture the official NOAA criteria used when categorizing and naming tropical storms and hurricanes (i.e., tropical cyclones), which requires maximum sustained winds of 39 miles per hour or greater. NOAA officials told us that the agency will continue to follow its criteria in naming these types of storms.

Page 3

Introduction
(Continued)

- The act requires that the Department of Commerce's National Oceanic and Atmospheric Administration (NOAA) generate post-storm assessments within 90 days of a named tropical storm or hurricane that the NOAA Administrator, in consultation with the Secretary of Homeland Security, determines may reasonably constitute a threat to any portion of a coastal state, including U.S. territories.[3]

- Under the act, NOAA must ensure, to the greatest extent practicable, that each post-storm assessment has a degree of accuracy of not less than 90 percent. In addition, the NOAA Administrator is to certify the degree of accuracy for each post-storm assessment, including specific reference to any segments or geographic areas for which the assessment is less than 90 percent accurate.

[3]Specifically, a coastal state is defined as a U.S. state in, or bordering on, the Atlantic, Pacific, or Arctic Ocean, the Gulf of Mexico, Long Island Sound, or one or more of the Great Lakes. In addition, the definition of a coastal state includes Puerto Rico and the other U.S. territories.

Page 4

Introduction
(Continued)

- To generate post-storm assessments, the act requires NOAA to develop by regulation a post-storm model that replicates wind speeds, storm surge heights, and other measurements for the designated named storm. The post-storm model must be designed to generate post-storm assessments that have a degree of accuracy of not less than 90 percent for every indeterminate loss for which it is utilized.

- NOAA also is to identify federal and state efforts, as well as domestic private and academic efforts, that are capable of collecting the weather data (i.e., covered data) necessary to develop the post-storm model and assessment, evaluate their coverage gaps, and report to Congress a plan for collecting the covered data.

- The act further requires FEMA, in consultation with NOAA, to establish by rule a standard formula to determine and allocate wind losses and flood losses for claims involving indeterminate losses that uses NOAA's post-storm assessment; however, FEMA can only use the post-storm assessment if NOAA certifies that it has a degree of accuracy of not less than 90 percent in connection with the specific indeterminate loss for which the assessment and formula are used.

Page 5

GAO

Objectives

- The COASTAL Act mandates GAO to audit federal efforts to collect covered data.

- The act mandates GAO to submit a report on its audit findings by July 6, 2013, to the Committees on Banking, Housing, and Urban Affairs and on Commerce, Science, and Transportation of the U.S. Senate; and the Committees on Financial Services and on Science, Space, and Technology of the House of Representatives.

- During the course of our work, NOAA was still in the process of developing the post-storm model and determining which data collection efforts would be required. Based on discussions with the cognizant congressional committees, we determined our objectives were to examine

  - storm data collection efforts that NOAA has identified that may provide the covered data for the COASTAL Act storm model, and

  - the extent to which selected federal agencies collect cost information on their storm data collection efforts.

Page 6

Scope and Methodology

To examine storm data collection efforts that NOAA has identified that may provide the covered data for the COASTAL Act storm model:

- We reviewed COASTAL Act planning documents from an interagency work group that included NOAA and other agencies—the U.S. Geological Survey (USGS), U.S. Army Corps of Engineers (the Corps), and National Aeronautics and Space Administration (NASA)—with which the act required NOAA to consult. Among the documents we reviewed were descriptions that officials compiled on the agencies' observing systems (referred to in this review as data collection efforts).

- We interviewed officials from NOAA and the other agencies identified above, as well as FEMA, the U.S. Coast Guard, and the Office of the Federal Coordinator for Meteorology (OFCM), with which the act also required NOAA to consult.[4] In addition to the agencies identified in the COASTAL Act, we interviewed representatives from a university, a nonprofit organization, and a private company about their storm data collection efforts because they were identified in the COASTAL Act planning documents and during interviews with the federal agencies.

[4]OFCM is an interdepartmental office, within the Department of Commerce, established in 1964 to coordinate federal meteorological activities among various agencies.

Scope and Methodology
(Continued)

To examine the extent to which selected agencies collect cost information on their storm data collection efforts:

- We selected NOAA and USGS to focus on because in examining objective 1, we found that these agencies had certain data collection efforts that agency officials told us would likely be an important source of covered data.

- We reviewed budget and financial documentation for fiscal years 2012 and 2013 provided by NOAA and USGS for these storm data collection efforts.

- We interviewed agency officials from NOAA and USGS to identify the type of cost information available for these agencies' storm data collection efforts.

Page 8

Scope and Methodology
(Continued)

- Officials from the Departments of Commerce, Defense, Homeland Security, and the Interior; NASA; and OFCM reviewed a draft version of this presentation for factual accuracy. Commerce and the Interior provided technical clarifications, which we incorporated as appropriate.

Summary of Findings

- NOAA, in consultation with OFCM and other agencies, has identified federal and nonfederal storm data collection efforts that may provide the covered data for the COASTAL Act storm model. However, NOAA officials told us they will not know which specific efforts will be used until they develop the model. According to agency officials and representatives from nonfederal entities, efforts that can collect surface level water, wave, and wind measurements over land will likely provide important sources of data for the model. However, these officials and representatives said current surface level data collection efforts may not be sufficient for the model to achieve the highly accurate estimates needed for individual structures in all locations. For example, data are not currently collected on waves that occur over land on top of the storm surge.

- The selected agencies we reviewed—NOAA and USGS—do not collect cost information on specific types of storm data, such as wind speed or storm surge. Agency officials said their data collection efforts typically collect multiple types of storm or weather data, and cost information on these efforts is calculated for all data collected. The agencies then incorporate the cost information they collect on these efforts into the costs of major programs and projects, such as responding to a major hurricane.

Page 10

Background

- As shown in figure 1, the COASTAL Act contains a number of requirements and deliverables for NOAA and FEMA to help FEMA establish a standardized loss allocation system for evaluating wind and water losses.

- NOAA's post-storm model (Named Storm Event Model) is a key requirement because it will be used to generate the post-storm assessments.

- The post-storm model must be designed to generate post-storm assessments that have a degree of accuracy of not less than 90 percent for every indeterminate loss for which it is utilized. The act does not define 90 percent accuracy and does not specify how to measure it.

- According to NOAA officials, developing a model that can replicate storm measurements for an individual structure with not less than 90 percent accuracy represents a scientific and technical challenge because the agency does not currently possess the capability to model with this level of detail.

Background (continued)
Figure 1: Timeline of COASTAL Act Requirements

July 6, 2012 — The Consumer Option for an Alternative System to Allocate Losses Act of 2012 (COASTAL Act) was enacted, along with other provisions reauthorizing and reforming, the National Flood Insurance Program within the Moving Ahead for Progress in the 21st Century Act.

January 2, 2013 — The National Oceanic and Atmospheric Administration (NOAA), in consultation with the Office of the Federal Coordinator for Meteorology (OFCM), must identify all federal and state efforts and systems as well as domestic private and academic systems that are capable of collecting covered data (not later than 180 days after enactment).

April 2, 2013 — NOAA, in consultation with OFCM, must submit to Congress a plan for collecting the covered data necessary to develop the storm model and post-storm assessment, including any coverage gaps in the identified systems (not later than 270 days after enactment).

July 6, 2013 — NOAA must establish a database—called the Coastal Wind and Water Event Database—for the collection and compilation of covered data (not later than 1 year after enactment).

December 28, 2013 — NOAA must develop a post-storm model—called the Named Storm Event Model—by regulation and a protocol for collecting and assembling the covered data (not later than 540 days after enactment).

June 26, 2014 — The Federal Emergency Management Agency (FEMA), in consultation with NOAA, must establish by rule a standard formula—called the COASTAL Formula—to determine and allocate wind losses and flood losses for claims involving indeterminate loss properties. Along with other information, the COASTAL Formula must use NOAA's post-storm assessment, if NOAA certifies that it has a degree of accuracy of not less than 90 percent in connection with the specific indeterminate loss for which the assessment and formula are used (not later than 180 days after NOAA establishes the protocol for collecting and assembling the covered data for the database).

FEMA must submit the COASTAL Formula to the National Academy of Sciences for evaluation; the National Academy will submit a report on this evaluation to congressional committees (upon issuance of the rule establishing the COASTAL Formula and any subsequent amendments).

Note: After FEMA establishes the COASTAL Formula, by rule, the NOAA Administrator, in consultation with the Secretary of Homeland Security, is required to identify named storms that may reasonably constitute a threat to any portion of a coastal state, as defined in the act (which includes U.S. territories). In addition, not later than 90 days after the identification of a named storm, NOAA must submit the post-storm assessment to the Secretary of Homeland Security.

Source: GAO analysis of the COASTAL Act.

Page 12

Background
(Continued)

- Under the act, NOAA's post-storm model must use covered data to replicate the condition of winds and water for a designated named tropical storm or hurricane.

- Covered data are specified in the act as data collected before, during, or after designated named storms and necessary to determine magnitude and timing of wind speeds, rainfall, barometric pressure, and river flows; the extent, height, and timing of storm surge; topographic (land shape) and bathymetric (ocean depth) data; and other measures.

- In addition to NOAA, a number of federal agencies collect weather data for diverse agency purposes. The act directs NOAA to consult with certain of these agencies—including USGS, the Corps, and NASA, among others—to coordinate the collection and maintenance of covered data and establish a process to share information regarding the covered data.

Page 13

Background
(Continued)

- In September 2012, OFCM established an interagency work group, co-chaired by NOAA, USGS, and the Corps, to help NOAA identify federal and nonfederal data collection efforts for purposes of the COASTAL Act. NOAA also solicited input from academic, state, and private entities.

- In consultation with the interagency work group, NOAA and OFCM developed a COASTAL Act Capabilities Development Plan to describe NOAA's approach for addressing the requirements of the act. At the time of our review, NOAA officials told us that the agency's senior leadership was reviewing the plan and the agency had not yet submitted the plan to Congress. Because it is unknown how long the entire clearance process will take, program officials do not know when the plan will be submitted to Congress.

- The plan identifies, among other things, the types of data it may need for its post-storm model. It also provides an inventory of federal and nonfederal weather data collection efforts that currently may collect the covered data at various levels of detail.

Page 14

Objective 1: Storm Data Collection Efforts

NOAA has identified storm data collection efforts that may provide the covered data for the post-storm model.

- NOAA, in consultation with OFCM and the other agencies in the interagency work group, identified a range of data collection efforts that may provide the covered data.

- These included data collection efforts by at least six federal agencies, as well as nonfederal entities. These efforts collect weather data on the ground and in water, as well as from sensors dropped from airplanes and positioned on satellites. For example, some NOAA airplanes fly into the eye of a hurricane and drop sensors to collect wind and other types of weather data.

- NOAA officials told us that the agency will not know which specific data collection efforts will be used or whether additional efforts would be needed until the agency develops the post-storm model. However, according to NOAA officials, there will be gaps in current data collection efforts. These gaps are discussed in more detail later in these slides.

**GAO**

Objective 1: Storm Data Collection Efforts
(Continued)

Surface Level Data Collection Efforts

- According to agency officials and representatives from nonfederal entities we spoke with, data collection efforts that can provide surface level water, wave, and wind measurements over land will likely provide important data for the post-storm model.

- These efforts will be important because the post-storm model will require measurements of water, wave, and wind data analyzed at regularly spaced time intervals (i.e., time series) as near as possible to the location of indeterminate loss structures.

- NOAA and USGS, as well as some nonfederal entities, such as universities and private companies, currently collect some surface level data on wind and water.

- The following two slides provide examples of surface level data collection efforts.

Page 16

GAO

Objective 1: Storm Data Collection Efforts
(Continued)

- **NOAA National Water Level Observation Network (NWLON):** These are permanent observing stations that, among other things, collect water level data at the coastline (see fig. 2). There are currently 210 NWLON stations nationwide, and 91 of these are located in states along the Gulf or East Coasts, as well as Puerto Rico and the U.S. Virgin Islands.

Figure 2: National Water Level Observation Network Station

Source: National Oceanic and Atmospheric Administration/ National Ocean Service/Center for Operational Oceanographic Products and Services.

- **USGS Mobile Storm Tide Networks:** These are mobile, temporary water level sensors that are installed along the shore line and a short distance inland (see fig. 3). There are 300 sensors distributed among USGS offices in most of the coastal states to facilitate rapid deployment 48 to 24 hours prior to a major storm's landfall. These sensors supplement permanent water level sensors.

Figure 3: U.S. Geological Survey (USGS) Storm Tide Sensor Deployed Prior to Hurricane Irene

Source: USGS/Photographer Kristen McSwain.

Page 17

GAO

Objective 1: Storm Data Collection Efforts
(Continued)

- **NOAA Automated Surface Observing Systems (ASOS):** This is a network of about 1,000 permanent stations located primarily at airports and operated jointly with the Federal Aviation Administration and Department of Defense (see fig. 4). ASOS stations measure wind speed and other weather data. There are about 145 stations located in coastal counties in the states along the Gulf and East Coasts, as well as Puerto Rico and U.S. Virgin Islands.

Figure 4: Automated Surface Observing Systems Station

Source: National Oceanic and Atmospheric Administration.

- **Digital Hurricane Consortium Deployable Sensors:** This is a network of mobile, temporary sensors, such as tripods called "StickNets," that collect wind speed and other weather data (see fig. 5). They are operated by a group of universities primarily in the Gulf Coast and Florida. These sensors are deployed on land at the expected location of a storm's landfall and aim to collect the highest wind speed.

Figure 5: Texas Tech University's "StickNet" Tripod

Source: Texas Tech University.

Page 18

Objective 1: Storm Data Collection Efforts
(Continued)

Gaps in Surface Level Data Collection Efforts

- According to agency officials and representatives from nonfederal entities we spoke with, current surface data collection efforts may not be sufficient for the post-storm model to achieve the highly accurate estimates needed for individual structures in all locations.

- For example, NOAA officials told us that wind speed sensors in ASOS are not designed to measure wind speeds greater than 190 miles per hour, which are the sustained wind speeds observed in the most severe category of hurricanes (i.e., Category 5). In addition, ASOS platforms are sometimes damaged or destroyed in major hurricanes. Furthermore, power failures during major storms often result in data losses from ASOS platforms. NOAA has been working to provide uninterrupted power supplies to a subset of ASOS stations located in hurricane-prone areas.

Objective 1: Storm Data Collection Efforts
(Continued)

- In addition, according to USGS officials, they may not have enough mobile storm tide sensors to deploy along the Atlantic Coast. Because tracking the location of hurricane landfall along the Atlantic Coast is more challenging than for storms approaching the Gulf Coast, the officials explained that the agency may need more sensors available in more locations along the Atlantic Coast.

- Further, NOAA officials told us storm data collection capabilities in the U.S. territories in the Caribbean and Pacific basins are extremely limited. The officials said that some locations may have only one or two storm data collection stations, and would need additional stations to adequately collect data on named storms in these locations.

Page 20

Objective 1: Storm Data Collection Efforts
(Continued)

- Officials from NOAA, USGS, and the Corps told us that current surface level data collection efforts do not measure certain types of data that likely will be needed to model wind and water impacts on individual structures. In particular, data on the action of waves that occur over land on top of the storm surge are critical for assessing water damage to structures from tropical storms and hurricanes but are not currently collected.

- Figure 6 in the following slide shows the different water level data needed to model storm surge, storm tide, and waves over land, according to agency officials.

  - Storm surge: an abnormal rise of water generated by a storm, above and beyond the normal high tide (data measured);

  - Storm tide: water level rise due to the combination of storm surge and the normal high tide (data measured);

  - Waves over land on top of storm surge (data not measured).

Objective 1: Storm Data Collection Efforts
(Continued)

Figure 6: Data Needed to Model Storm Surge, Storm Tide, and Waves Over Land

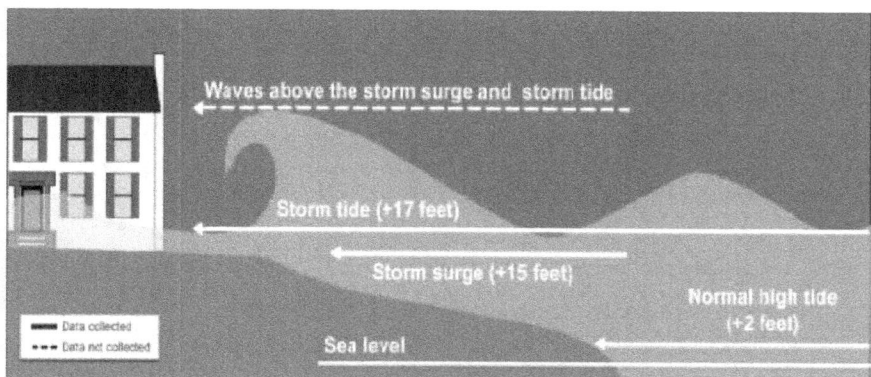

Source: National Oceanic and Atmospheric Administration.

Objective 1: Storm Data Collection Efforts
(Continued)

<u>Topographic and Bathymetric Data Collection Efforts</u>

- According to NOAA officials, data on land shape and ocean depth (i.e., topographic and bathymetric data) will be needed to replicate conditions at an individual structure.

- NOAA, USGS, and the Corps collect these data for different purposes. For example:

  - NOAA collects bathymetric data from coastal and open ocean areas in support of mission requirements, including charting, navigation, and hazard mitigation, as well as for storm surge forecast models.

  - USGS collects topographic and bathymetric data to study the vulnerability of U.S. shorelines to coastal change hazards such as the effects of severe storms.

  - The Corps collects topographic and bathymetric data of U.S. shorelines to support design of specific projects, operations, dredging, and regulatory functions.

- According to agency officials, the agencies collect these data through both individual and joint efforts.

Page 23

Objective 1: Storm Data Collection Efforts
(Continued)

Gaps in Topographic and Bathymetric Data

- NOAA officials told us that current topographic and bathymetric data of U.S. coastal areas may be outdated because of significant coastline changes due to erosion and other factors.

- In addition, NOAA officials also told us that these data must first be processed into a digital elevation model in order to be used as input data in storm models; however, current high-quality digital elevation models that would likely be needed for the post-storm model are not available for all U.S. coastal areas, in particular the Gulf and East Coasts.

- NOAA officials told us that the agency has produced most of its current high-quality digital elevation models to support the agency's Tsunami Program, primarily on the West Coast, Alaska, Hawaii, and the Caribbean. NOAA uses data from federal and other sources, and coordinates development of these models with the State-Federal National Tsunami Hazard Mitigation Program.

Page 24

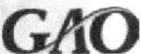

Objective 1: Storm Data Collection Efforts
(Continued)

- In addition to topographic and bathymetric data, NOAA officials told us that related data on land use and cover (e.g., residential areas or forests) will be needed to replicate wind conditions for an individual structure. Specifically, these data are converted to "roughness" data which determines how different types of land use and cover affect wind speed and direction.

- NOAA officials told us that highly detailed roughness data will be needed for analyzing wind for the post-storm model. However, the officials explained that such data are not currently available for U.S. coastal areas susceptible to tropical storms and hurricanes.

Page 25

Objective 1: Storm Data Collection Efforts
(Continued)

- Agency officials told us that although their current storm data collection efforts collect similar types of data, the data have important differences and supplement each other for purposes of measuring storm conditions. For example:

  - NOAA's permanent, fixed NWLON stations, which are located miles apart along the U.S. coast, measure water levels at all times for multiple purposes and not solely for observing major storms.

  - USGS's mobile storm tide sensors are typically positioned during major storms to supplement data collected by NOAA's fixed water level sensors to obtain detailed measures of the advancing storm surge.

- NOAA officials told us that, among their next steps in planning for meeting the requirements of the COASTAL Act, the agency will be examining how to fill the gaps they identified in current storm data collection efforts.

Page 26

Objective 2: Cost Information

Agencies do not collect cost information that reflects the costs of all activities in collecting and using a specific type of storm data.

- The selected agencies we reviewed—NOAA and USGS—do not typically collect cost information for each type of storm or weather data, such as wind speed or storm surge, that reflects the expense for all activities involved in collecting and using the data. For example:

  - NOAA officials told us that they do not track a cost figure that reflects the costs of all activities involved in collecting and using a unit of wind speed data from their ASOS stations.

- Agency officials told us that the following activities involved in collecting storm data generate costs: deployment, maintenance, and operation of observing systems; communications and processing; analysis; dissemination; and data storage.

Page 27

Objective 2: Cost Information
(Continued)

- Officials from NOAA and USGS told us that their storm data collection efforts generally involve more than one type of storm or weather data.

- The costs for processing, analyzing, and storing the data are calculated for all data types rather than a single one. For example:

  - NOAA officials told us that their NWLON stations collect data on water levels, wind, and barometric pressure. NOAA officials told us that it would be challenging, for example, to identify the costs for processing only the water level data because agency staff process all data collected by the NWLON stations at the same time.

  - NOAA officials also told us that data storage is a centralized agency activity provided by the National Environmental Satellite, Data, and Information Service. The costs for the staff and computing resources needed are based on all storm data types and not one element of data.

Page 28

Objective 2: Cost Information
(Continued)

- Agencies incorporate the cost information they collect on their storm data collection efforts into the costs of major programs and projects.

- According to NOAA officials, the agency's major programs include the costs of multiple storm data collection efforts. For example, one official told us that cost information is collected for all data from NWLON stations and another effort under one program.

- NOAA and USGS officials told us that they also collect cumulative cost information for special projects, such as activities related to responding to a major hurricane.

  - USGS officials collected detailed cost information on storm tide, barometric pressure, and high water mark level data collected during Hurricane Sandy.[5] USGS reported total costs for all activities, such as deploying and operating sensors, and processing and disseminating the data, were about $533,000.

- As a next step in its COASTAL Act planning, NOAA plans to prepare a resource analysis that is to, in part, identify some of the additional resources needed to fill gaps in storm data collection efforts.

[5]USGS's storm tide data collection effort for Hurricane Sandy was funded by FEMA.

Page 29

Enclosure II

GAO Contact and Staff Acknowledgements

GAO Contact

Anne-Marie Fennell, (202) 512-3841 or fennella@gao.gov

Staff Acknowledgements

In addition to the contact listed above, key contributors to this report were Jeff Malcolm, Assistant Director; Cheryl Arvidson; Brian M. Friedman; Cindy Gilbert; Bridget Grimes; Armetha Liles; Mehrzad Nadji; and Jeanette Soares.

(361445)

GAO's Mission	The Government Accountability Office, the audit, evaluation, and investigative arm of Congress, exists to support Congress in meeting its constitutional responsibilities and to help improve the performance and accountability of the federal government for the American people. GAO examines the use of public funds; evaluates federal programs and policies; and provides analyses, recommendations, and other assistance to help Congress make informed oversight, policy, and funding decisions. GAO's commitment to good government is reflected in its core values of accountability, integrity, and reliability.
Obtaining Copies of GAO Reports and Testimony	The fastest and easiest way to obtain copies of GAO documents at no cost is through GAO's website (www.gao.gov). Each weekday afternoon, GAO posts on its website newly released reports, testimony, and correspondence. To have GAO e-mail you a list of newly posted products, go to www.gao.gov and select "E-mail Updates."
Order by Phone	The price of each GAO publication reflects GAO's actual cost of production and distribution and depends on the number of pages in the publication and whether the publication is printed in color or black and white. Pricing and ordering information is posted on GAO's website, http://www.gao.gov/ordering.htm. Place orders by calling (202) 512-6000, toll free (866) 801-7077, or TDD (202) 512-2537. Orders may be paid for using American Express, Discover Card, MasterCard, Visa, check, or money order. Call for additional information.
Connect with GAO	Connect with GAO on Facebook, Flickr, Twitter, and YouTube. Subscribe to our RSS Feeds or E-mail Updates. Listen to our Podcasts. Visit GAO on the web at www.gao.gov.
To Report Fraud, Waste, and Abuse in Federal Programs	Contact: Website: www.gao.gov/fraudnet/fraudnet.htm E-mail: fraudnet@gao.gov Automated answering system: (800) 424-5454 or (202) 512-7470
Congressional Relations	Katherine Siggerud, Managing Director, siggerudk@gao.gov, (202) 512-4400, U.S. Government Accountability Office, 441 G Street NW, Room 7125, Washington, DC 20548
Public Affairs	Chuck Young, Managing Director, youngc1@gao.gov, (202) 512-4800 U.S. Government Accountability Office, 441 G Street NW, Room 7149 Washington, DC 20548

Please Print on Recycled Paper.